A Penny for your thoughts

Written by

Norman O'Neill

Profits from the sale of this book will go to
the charity Painting with Penny.

Contents

Sister Wendy Becket

The famous quotation, 'Man is born free, but is everywhere in chains', was made in a political context, but it has a deeper meaning. We are all too often enchained by our natural anxieties and frustrations, by financial troubles, by relationships, sickness, mental illnesses.

Few people would claim that they are truly 'free'. Art does not offer us an escape from life's difficulties, but it does show us how to set struggle or pain in their place: they are partial, there is more. Through art, we can reach out to what is deepest in us, to joy and creativity.

Beauty abides whatever the distress around it. And in accepting the enlargement of spirit that beauty represents, we become our real selves, who are not meant to be circumscribed by distress, but to use that is painful so as to reach our destined and unique integrity.

Norman O'Neill began painting in 1995 in order to support his daughter Penny who suffers from a schizophrenic illness. He had never painted before. Penny, as her father says, 'has proved to be a lovely artist.'

These brave, bright pictures, with their immensely sympathetic response to the world of nature, their obvious pleasure in what is seen, their contemplative readiness to look, to look long, and then express what has been experienced in visual terms, are a heart-warming sign of the importance - the transforming importance - of art.

Sister Wendy Beckett   1997

Thank you for looking at this, my book. I want you to open your mind and think. Mental illness is a subject rarely talked about; we are conditioned from early childhood to mock and ridicule those who do not conform. Innocent playground jokes, games and traditions set in our minds those prejudices that can so haunt us in later life.

History gives us countless examples of people who excelled, despite being unable to live in harmony with their fellow citizens. Self-expression through art is discovered in childhood and cast aside as we grow older and mature. Were they mentally ill? What is normality? Countries, races, religions all impose patterns of behaviour on the lives of their people. Out of context, they may seem out of place. Who are we to judge what is normal and what is not?

We were the most normal of families, hard working, honest and decent, yet through the illness of my daughter Penny, we have come to understand the realities of mental illness; we have experienced despair and witnessed hope.

Share with me my story and rejoice with me in the wonderful paintings that have emerged from our torment. Art has enabled us to express our feelings in a way that we could not otherwise have done. Words themselves, cannot describe our experiences as we have fought together to conquer mental illness - and believe me, we are not alone!

Chapter One   Dawn

You can perhaps be forgiven, for thinking that mental illness could never strike your family. After all, you're all normal aren't you? In common with most of us, I too thought that mental illness was something that happened in other families. Yes, I gave to those who shook a tin and sold a flag. I also looked the other way, when someone's behaviour in the street was clearly the product of some inner torment or learning disability.

Of course we never take the trouble to understand the difference between mental illness and mental disability. If someone has a problem in that department, we group them all together. In fact in my youth, they were usually locked away, in some bleak institution. Out of sight and certainly out of mind.

But, you might be saying, this chap Norman O'Neill is not like us. His family has suffered mental illness. Let me tell you something about myself and my family. Although penned under a pseudonym, this is purely to protect Penny. Honest, frank and brutally open there's no embellishment and certainly no fabrication in the story I am telling you.

For generations, my family have lived and worked on the North Yorkshire Moors. I was born there into a heritage of proud tradition. My parents continued that heritage, giving us a very sound upbringing where we knew our place and what was expected as we went through life. In those days, before the Second World War, life had changed little in centuries.

Purchased Caravan 1953

'Home sweet home'
ANON

Our family had strong links with Fountains Abbey at Ripon and like the Abbey, had weathered the passing years virtually unchanged. We were not wealthy, not famous and everything we had we'd worked hard for.

On leaving school in the mid 1940s, I was apprenticed at a local building firm where I worked for seven years, learning my trade. Like all in my generation I did National Service and perhaps like most other young men in those days, my two years in the RAF gave me my first real experience of life outside the area where I had been born and bred.

Back in Yorkshire, a little older and a lot wiser, I returned to construction and fell in love with a local dress fitter Rosemary. Her background had been similar to mine and we had much in common. Poverty was one of them!

We saved hard to buy our first home which I have recently painted for you.

Yes, we started our married life in a caravan which we parked in a field belonging to a friendly farmer who recognised our plight and understood our desire to start our married life in our own home, albeit a very small one. We baby sat for him and his wife in lieu of ground rent.

Oriental Poppies

'If it were not for hopes, the heart would break'
THOMAS FULLER (1608-1661)

Ironically, for the past twenty years I have made my living selling caravans, often to couples who like Rosemary and I, wanted a cheap place in which to start their married life.

Our caravan was nothing like the luxury 'mobile homes' I sell today. No loo or electricity, we had just two small gas rings to heat water, cook food and try to drive away the cold, penetrating damp. Made of hardboard with a canvas roof, you can imagine what it was like.

We had five daughters in all and no sons. When the first was born, we moved out of the caravan and lived with Rosemary's mother at Thirsk, losing all of the money we had invested in the caravan - it was impossible to sell it.

When our second child was born, we moved into a council house and stayed there for many years until my career progressed to a point where we could afford a mortgage. Then, we borrowed what seemed then an awful lot of money and moved to Richmond, Yorkshire. We were very proud of our first house and Penny was born there. A successful career led us to move south in the early '70s and our last daughter was born away from our Yorkshire roots.

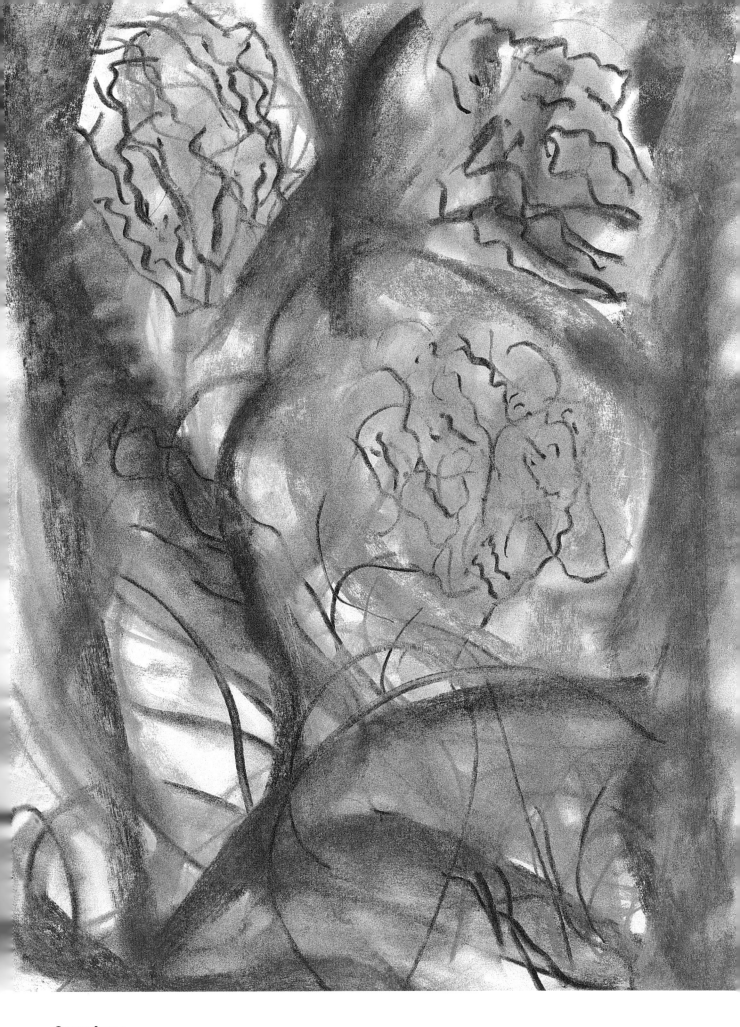

Geraniums

'Say it with flowers'.
PATRICK O'KEEFE

Life was good in those days; we were still very much in love and had five wonderful daughters. All were happy, healthy and growing fast - what more could I have wanted? Perhaps you're like that right now, content with life, established in a comfortable relationship with your family around you.

Rather like those early days of my life in the late 1930s, the good times were too good to last and in 1982 the peace was abruptly broken . . .

Horses

'Action is eloquence'.
WILLIAM SHAKESPEARE

Chapter Two   Thunder

Thunder

Unlike the growing political tension of the late 1930s, we had no warning that our war with mental illness was about to break out. Life was good; I had a good wife and five wonderful daughters and a flourishing career. What more could a man ask for?

We liked our new home in the south a lot and when asked to take a promotion and move to London, I decided to stay where I was and work for myself. I worked hard and perhaps with hindsight would have spent more time with the family in those days, but the pressure was on me to earn a living and build a business. I'm sure many of you reading this can relate to that situation.

It was summer 1983 and my family was blossoming. Boyfriends, exams, late nights and yes, you could never get in the bathroom - I felt at peace with the world and content with my lot. Penny had always been a quiet girl and was studying hard for her 'O' levels. She attended the comprehensive school in the nearby town where my business was based, and although mostly happy, suffered a bit from bullying at the hands of her classmates.

I had no idea what tensions were building up in the mind of my Penny at that time - or how they would come to haunt our family for years and years.

Penny and my wife Rosemary went up to Yorkshire to visit relatives whilst the rest of the family remained with me in Norfolk. It was early summer and they stayed with Rosemary's sister near Northallerton. There, without warning Penny's health broke and within the space of one hour, the daughter we loved and cherished left us to be replaced by someone we had never met before, but were to come to know only too well. Schizophrenia had arrived.

Plantation Gardens

'Life is a pure flame, and we live by an invisible sun within us'.
SIR THOMAS BROWN

Penny spent six weeks in Darlington hospital before she was well enough to come home; Rosemary stayed with her, whilst I worried at home and looked after our other daughters. You cannot begin to imagine the despair I felt at that time. What had we done wrong? What could we have done differently? How could I have prevented my Penny from suffering in this way? Many nights were spent awake, staring at the ceiling, trying to understand what had gone wrong.

When Penny returned, I was shocked by how much she had changed; by the extent to which she seemed influenced by people she couldn't see and we could never know; the anxiety, frustration, the tears. The very destructive nature of the disease that had invaded her head and destroyed the sweet innocence of her youth was frightening. She had matured and changed - yet she was still our daughter and needed our love all the more - how difficult it was to understand.

As the weeks passed, we became accustomed to Penny's illness, although it did not make it any easier to cope with. Her rejection of the standards of attitude and behaviour that we had always accepted as 'normal' were deeply distressing - especially to Rosemary, my wife. Penny would spend most of the day in bed, then in the evening, when we were worn out from a day at work, she would get up and want to go out, do the garden, wash the car, visit friends. With tremendous feelings of guilt, we often used to let her do just as she pleased, because as we came to appreciate, those offers of help were in fact tremendous achievements, despite appearing more than a little eccentric. Tell me; how do you reason with someone whose perception of normality is so different from our own?

Pleasant dreams

After C. Cochrane

'The block of granite which was an obstacle to the weak, became a stepping stone of the strong'.
THOMAS CARLYLE

Our family doctor was some comfort, although he, like us was shocked by the changes in our daughter. The specialists at the local hospital talked us through the illness, what it was, how it was so little understood, yet surprisingly common. Were they really talking about our Penny? We struggled to find the answers ourselves - but our search was hampered by the misconceptions and fears that inhibit us all when faced with mental illness.

Reflecting on my own childhood, when our country was at war, I realised that my own parents must have suffered the same anxiety, questioning the uncertainties that accompany war. Like them, we did not know what the future held and when we asked, we encountered busy people who had told the story many times before. I had to pinch myself because it felt like I wasn't really there - the presentations were delivered with feeling and sympathy, but were just too polished to be meant just for us. Is this what mental illness is really all about?

Let me take you back there with me to those haunting meetings with the psychiatrists when we were told about our Penny's illness. For a start, they were held in the local mental hospital, a dark and forbidding place where despite the best efforts of the friendly staff, you could be forgiven for thinking you had returned to a Dickensian work-house. (In fact I found out years later that underneath that hospital are the cellars where the insane used to be chained!)

Ashcroft flowers

'Take rest; a field that has rested gives a beautiful crop'.
OVID

At the first meeting, we were told all about schizophrenia, that it was actually quite common and about some of the changes that we had noticed in Penny that seemed so difficult to understand and explain. For example, she seemed to turn inwards and shut us all out, she wouldn't take part in family activities and lost interest in almost everything. The doctor there told us that schizophrenia was a common affliction, caused by chemical changes within the brain. Why then, can't it be cured as quickly as other physical complaints? We left that meeting with heavy hearts - why, oh why did this happen to us?

Later meetings did little to reassure us. We heard about some really frightening symptoms that we knew only too well were affecting our Penny. Reality and imagination get muddled and confused; voices seem real, even though they don't exist; emotions get reversed and our Penny would laugh at adversity and cry at delight.

You can't imagine the despair we felt, the anguish, the hurt and above all else, the tremendous feeling of guilt. What could we have done differently to make things turn out any other way?

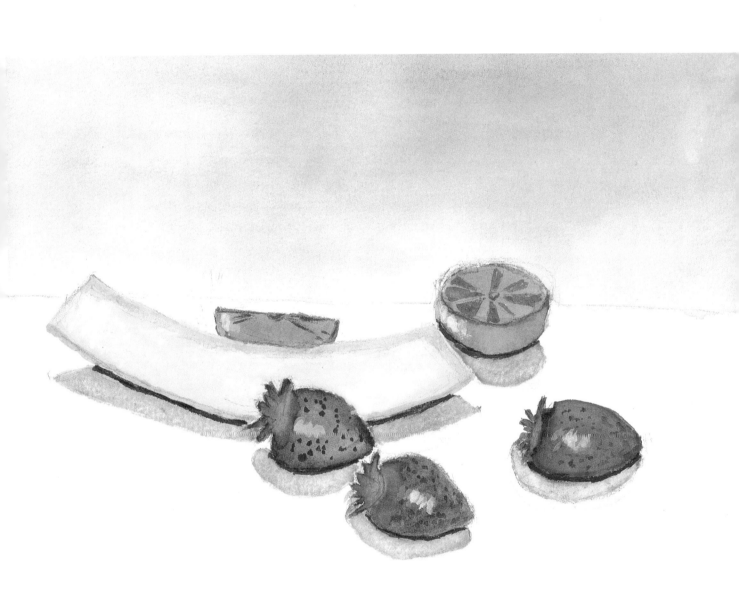

Small oranges

"The first attempts are absolutely unbearable"
VINCENT VAN GOGH

Our next visit to the hospital gave us a few more answers. Schizophrenia can be inherited, but is more influenced by personality and the individual's ability to cope. Stress in small quantities is good for you, but too much, if you are susceptible, can literally tip you over the edge. That trip to Yorkshire, meant to celebrate Penny leaving school may well have been the straw that broke the camel's back. The stress of staying away from the security of her home, on top of the worry associated with the changes involved with leaving school, were just too much. It makes you realise just how fragile that state we call 'normality' actually is.

Our third meeting with those men in white coats gave as more hope. Our Penny was responding well to treatment and was beginning to get back some of her old sparkle and vitality. As the Doctor explained, schizophrenia was like diabetes; Penny must continue treatment long after the symptoms disappear. Was it really as simple as that? No of course not. There was much more to follow as the weeks turned into months and even years.

Remembrance

After S. Bull

'*There are certain things we feel to be beautiful and good, and we must hunger after them*'.
GEORGE ELLIOT (1819 -1880)

Chapter Three   Rainbows

32

Imagine for a moment that you are out in the countryside. It's a bright day, perhaps in Spring and the leaves on the trees are just unfurling. The grass is green and lush and the cattle are out in the meadows around your village. You go for a walk along a long grassy track, perhaps with a friend. The sky darkens and it begins to rain. You shelter under a tree.

The storm soon passes and as the sun comes out, a rainbow appears, forming a vivid arc from earth to sky. You could almost reach out and touch it and walk out from under the trees with their brilliant green, wet leaves glistening in the sun towards that captivating beam of colour. The earth smells fresh and the cows are grazing contentedly on the other side of the hedge. Then, suddenly, the rainbow disappears and more clouds blot out the sun. It begins to rain, slowly at first, then harder. Another storm; a roll of thunder; that dear reader, is schizophrenia.

The intensity of those Spring colours, fresh and moist. The desire to touch a rainbow, so bright and surreal. The frustration when it disappears and disappoints you.

'Was it really there? Why did it seem so real? Didn't you see it too Dad?' 'Yes my darling, I saw it, but I know it's just a show - pictures, colours, images in the sky'. Why then, is it that we can see the rainbow, smell the electricity in the air, hear the rumble of thunder and crack of lightning - why can't we reach out and make it our own?

View from the Wheatfield II

After Van Gogh

'We shall fight them in the fields'.
WINSTON CHURCHILL

That is the puzzle of schizophrenia. We all know that rainbows are not real, cannot be touched, preserved, yet we see them. It's rather like the thirst crazed traveller lost in the desert. He can see the water through the shimmering haze above the golden sand under the blazing rays of the sun. His fellow travellers can see it too and with equal enthusiasm they throw themselves towards it, yet as we all know, it's a mirage - it's not really there at all. We call this normality. Can you wonder that the ill become confused!

Of course science tells us that these phenomena are easily explained. The sun reflecting from water droplets in the air and that a mirage is an optical illusion. Nature playing games with our eyes. How then, can the phenomenon I've come to know as schizophrenia be explained? I read lots of books and asked lots of questions. I was determined to understand. To our Penny, life was full of rainbows and shimmering mirages. She saw things that we could not, but which to her were as real as those rainbows we saw together. She heard voices, deep inside her head - think about it - we are really all restricted by the limitations of the bodies we are born with. Science has progressed, but the human body has not developed at all in 2,000 years. No wonder it plays up sometimes.

"You guess"

'Guessing so much and so much'.
G K CHESTERTON

Putting schizophrenia into context is important. You need to understand that there's nothing new about it - except perhaps that we now can recognise, diagnose and treat this awful illness that corrupts the harmony between man and his environment, changes it, disturbs it and makes everything seem a little out of sync.

In our so-called civilised society, madness or insanity was not regarded as a health problem until around 1800. Those who did not conform were isolated and restrained. Chained in those dreadful cellars that remain beneath the hospital where Penny was treated. Of course physicians were little better informed and death was the inevitable outcome of many of those illnesses now considered trivial. In the absence of anaesthetics, alcohol, brute force and sparing amounts of sympathy were the best that most could find and even the richest in the land could not benefit from the relief afforded by even the simplest antibiotic until well into the twentieth century.

Believe it or not no one recognised schizophrenia as a unique condition until 1911 when the Swiss psychiatrist Dr Eugen Bleuler first used the term to distinguish it from the more severe depressive illnesses he had studied.

Adolescence, that turbulent, roller coaster ride from childhood to maturity is the most common time for the problem to surface. Understandably, the hormonal and emotional changes that are part of growing up, together with the inevitable questioning of self and sense, can literally 'tip over the edge' the susceptible young person.

Earth Wind and Fire

'Winning starts with beginning'.
ROBERT SCHULER

The academics and researchers have spent millions trying to identify those factors that can predispose a youngster to become schizophrenic, but rather like predicting heart disease in later life, the calculation becomes actuarial rather than factual. The research does not seem to have been done, and what has been analysed cannot always be easily explained.

Despite the lack of knowledge, schizophrenia is probably the most common mental illness with around one per cent of the world's population estimated to be affected. When you reckon that most sufferers are aged between 15 to 25, that must mean that around one adolescent in twenty will suffer in this way. How many sufferers do you know? You must know at least one - but then of course the symptoms don't show in the same way as a broken arm - there's no plaster cast on which to sign your name!

Fear, is the biggest stigma that affects the sufferer. Social ignorance and a general unwillingness to understand push the schizophrenic deeper into themselves. Their friends may share the rainbows and the mirage, but find it hard to look deeper and recognise that reality is a perceptive condition, not fact. Sorry if I sound a little philosophical, but consider this. To the Amazonian Indian, termites are tastier than a fast food burger. To the blind person, colour may be perceived quite clearly and vividly, yet never be actually seen. To our Penny, the voices in her head were as real as if you or I were standing right beside her. Believe me, to her they were real; what right have we to question that?

Please don't put the book down on your lap and say that this couldn't ever happen in your family; the figures should tell you that it could, it might and if you're a statistician, you'll appreciate that the odds are that one day, it most probably will!

Butterfly Lady

'There is no heavier burden than a great potential'.
CHARLIE BROWN

40

There has been research conducted that indicates that children of people with schizophrenia have a 10 per cent chance of contracting the illness themselves, that's ten times the global average. Problem is, no one knows why that is. Studies of twins, where one twin contracted schizophrenia, showed that identical (genetically) twins were more likely to also suffer than non-identical twins. What's more, studies of adopted children shows that the pre-disposition to schizophrenia is influenced by the parents' genes, not the adoptive parents' behaviour. In other words, the problem can be proved to be genetically influenced more than environmentally.

Why so serious? Well if your child became ill in this way, the natural instinct is to blame yourself. To question your lifestyle and to punish yourself by remembering all those things you wish you had done, but at the time, were just too busy (in my case, working).

These findings were very reassuring to me. As I said earlier, we came from a hard working, very traditional Yorkshire family where being ill meant being physically ill. Subtle changes to the brain were hard to understand and harder to explain. However, unlike our forefathers, we strove to understand, we read, we asked, we explored. As time went by, we began to understand and as we understood, we realised how difficult it was to express our feelings for this thing that had blighted our existence. Penny and I began to paint.

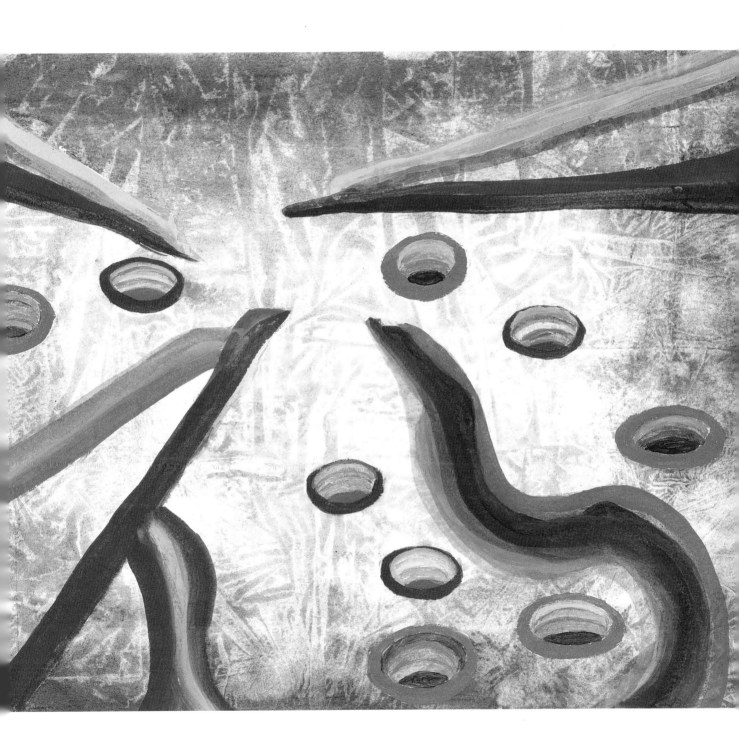

What's happening

'Painting is how you feel at the time'.
NORMAN O'NEILL

Chapter Four   Shadows

The expression of our feelings through the medium of art took some practice. After all, we all paint as children when we are at school, then grow up believing that only children and artists paint. Believe me, nothing could be further from the truth.

Self-belief is everything and if you want to be an artist, you can. Let me prove it to you. Put this book down for a while and draw a picture of something that means a lot to you. Think about it and why it's so important as you draw. Perhaps you will want to draw a favourite place, or somewhere you would like to have been. Remember for example Constable's 'Hay Wain', a picture of tranquillity beside a meandering East Anglian river, painted in the Spring. If you have children, borrow their coloured pencils and use those. Use whatever you can find. It won't be easy to start with, but after you make those first few faint lines with your pencil, the rest will gradually follow The picture that is in your mind will slowly emerge and take shape on the paper before you. Now stand back and look at what you've achieved. My guess is that, not only will you be pleasantly surprised by what you've achieved, you will feel much more contented too. Now, that image that was in your mind, has been translated into a form that others can share and see with you.

One of the features of our so-called civilised society is that we are conditioned to expect failure if we veer from the predicted path. Teachers teach, farmers farm, salesmen sell and artists paint. Or do they? Let me cast some shadows over this myth that we have to conform and cannot excel in spheres other than our own. One of the tragedies of modern society is that we are often categorised and expected to be what our parents, teachers, friends and colleagues expect us to be. Go on, rebel a little - you will enjoy being yourself.

Sunflowers II

After Van Gogh

'Pride is a flower that's free'
NOEL COWARD

Shadows

Vincent Van Gogh was just such a non-conformist. He was born in the Dutch region of Brabant in March 1853. His father was a pastor in the Dutch Reform Church and as we all know, his paintings, of which perhaps the most famous is called 'Sunflowers', hangs in the Van Gogh museum in Amsterdam. Any art expert will tell you that Van Gogh is one of the world's greatest painters.

What people don't say about Van Gogh, is that he was a real person too, who only turned to painting because he could not pass the necessary exams to study theology. We all chose to remember Van Gogh for what he became, not as a man who had a whole spectrum of interests, concerns, fears and emotions.

n 1873 he was a shy, awkward twenty-year-old, living in a foreign company working as an apprentice to an international firm of art dealers. His uncle had fixed him up with a job in the firm he managed when young, Vincent left school. He had always been a quiet child, preferring his own company to that of others. His very introspective nature and the dogmatic views of his strict father must have made him an easy target for playground bullies at his school. (Although we will never know if this is true!).

If I told you that this Dutch lad was living in a boarding house in Clapham and spent his spare time walking in London's great parks and reading the writings of contemporaries such as Charles Dickens, you might be forgiven for thinking that I had forgotten that we were discussing Van Gogh. No, Vincent Van Gogh (known as Vince perhaps to his London colleagues) was far from famous at that time and led a very lonely life, exploring the places that we all visit today when we go to London. Does he lose any of his mystique when I describe him to you in this way? Perhaps he does, but what I am telling you is the reality of his younger years. What are you doing with your life at the moment? What do you aspire to achieve? What are you waiting for!

900 Years

'The innocent and the beautiful have no enemy but time'
ANON

48

Think for a moment. Do you really think that Vincent Van Gogh expected to be world famous? Did he foresee the establishment of that great museum to house his work? No, of course he didn't. He painted to express his feelings, to pour out his thoughts and present them to the world through his brother and friends. For Van Gogh, painting was an outlet for his frustrations and fears. Fame was an unexpected consequence that in reality, only happened long after Van Gogh was dead and buried.

As I've described earlier, Penny and I took up painting for just the same reasons as Van Gogh. We wanted to share our feelings in a very visual way, for painting removes the restrictions of writing, where words have meanings and it is only too easy to be mis-understood. Music of course is another vehicle for self-expression, but unlike a painting, nothing remains without human intervention. When the flautist stops blowing or the violinist rests his arm, the music stops. For us, the permanence of our paintings is everything. We could not for example have shared music with you through the pages of this book.

Look at a picture and your brain and eye link to form impressions in your mind, free of perception and inference. For Penny and I, our paintings provide very clear windows, through which those who want to, can see right into our innermost thoughts.

Haystacks II

After Van Gogh

'So that's what hay looks like'.
QUEEN MARY

50

Remember too, that we are nothing more than an ordinary family, working hard and living reasonably well. Honest Yorkshire people with no pretensions to become famous artists. Far from it, I focused all of my attentions on building my business and really only stopped to think when I reached the age when most men are thinking of retiring.

Schizophrenia is the catalyst that sparks our creativity and drives us to paint. Penny, as the illness ebbs and flows, crashing around her mind like waves on a stormy beach, myself as I wrestle with the torment of witnessing my beloved daughter suffering as she does. Painting gives us a vehicle for sharing our feelings for each other and for sharing them with you too.

If you've studied art, you will know that Van Gogh suffered from schizophrenic illness. Like our Penny he was a quiet child, unhappy at school and from a family with strong principles and ethics. Like our Penny he suffered many breakdowns and resorted to painting to express his views.

Boats

'I have learned more from my mistakes than my successes'.
SIR HUMPHRY DAVY

It was only after we had been painting a few years that we realised the similarity in style. Van Gogh painted at a frenetic pace during 1889 when he was in the depths of schizophrenic depression. Four breakdowns in that year had a tremendous impact on this man, by then living in France. In the space of fifteen weeks he created 70 oil paintings and 30 watercolours. Think about it, that's virtually one painting every day for almost four months.

Imagine the powerful emotions that drove him to paint with such vigour and strength. That's the power of schizophrenia. The extremes of emotion, the vivid colours and daring designs - intense love, damming hate, the feelings alternate and drive the paint across the canvas.

Van Gogh's work at this time was vivid, colourful and as we know now, similar to that of others with the same illness. I wonder, how many of today's schizophrenic painters will one day be as famous as Van Gogh?

Birds

'An artist is a dreamer consenting to dream of the real world'.
GEORGE SANTAYANA

Chapter Five   Sunshine - Father

Prayer, say the mystics, is the lifting up of the mind and heart to God. The deepest, most mystical prayer of all is to be found in the calmness of contemplation and meditation. Salvation cannot result from besieging the Gates of Heaven with an endless shopping list of requests and demands. Little wonder, then, that so many of our prayers seem to go unheard and unheeded!

But meditating does not necessarily mean retreating to a lonely mountain peak or to a hermit's chapel. I have found my ideal state of inner communion with the infinite in my paintings and those of my daughter, Penny. That moment of awareness, that stillness of the soul when one looks not at an object, but into its very being before committing one's thoughts to paper, is surely one of the most profound and personal experiences in life. Yet Penny and I have only discovered its true worth within the last three or four years.

Had we discovered the soothing therapeutic aspect of art at the outset of our respective trials and traumas, who knows what benefits might by now have accrued to us as those benefits grow by compound interest.

'Art is no good, there's no money in that', was my forcefully given opinion when one or the other of my five daughters wanted to explore its possibilities for themselves. How wrong I was - with Penny's help, love and encouragement I have seen the golden rays of sunshine and painted them for all to see.

St Maarten

'Without deviation, progress is not possible'.
FRANK ZAPPA

Sunshine - Father

Now, we enjoy and share the benefits of tranquillity. Freed from the shackles of daily labour, I find true relaxation as I explore the meaning of life within each chosen subject, whether technically living or not. Through painting, I have brought that light and colour into my life which I had unknowingly craved throughout years of unremitting stress in the harsh commercial world, where every drop of blood, every puff of breath from our bodies is demanded of us.

But don't let me give the wrong impression. I have always enjoyed working hard, have willingly devoted my spare time and energy to learning new skills and studying the laws that govern our physical environment, even when the pressures of financial forces and family well being have temporarily caused my mind to temporarily shut down under the strain. If you want something done, ask a busy person, runs the old maxim, and that sums up the whole of my experience in life - until I took to painting.

Leaving school in my native Yorkshire village in 1943 - I was just 14 years old - I was apprenticed to a joiner and undertaker for seven long, (almost) unpaid years. In that wartime atmosphere, now almost to far away to remember, I worked long, hard hours. My effort and commitment meant that I soon found myself in charge of the shop when my employer was called away

I become highly skilled in the ways of woodworking, from boxes to carts, and still had time to become a Venture Scout. I followed the usual life of a teenager in the forties, a term we had not yet captured from the American forces, but which applied all the same!

Even during my RAF service from the age of 21, I managed to carry on with the scouting in the best of moonlighting traditions. During my two years service, mostly spent a few miles from home at RAF Leeming, I learned the trade of Air Wireless Mechanic; presumably, recruits from the wireless trade were made to study carpentry!

Mothers Day

'If it were not for hopes, the heart would break'.
THOMAS FULLER (1608 - 1661)

Chapter Five   Sunshine - Father

The future course of life was mapped out for me from the beginning of my demob
leave when I attended a friend's 21st birthday party and met my wife to be, Rosemary.
By the time that we were married, just over a year later, I was already a charge-hand
in a building firm. But where could we live in those days of post-war austerity?
Housing was scarce, money more so, the armed forces had been mainly discharged,
disgorging thousands of young hopefuls into civilian life, where the competition was
fierce for everything that one needed to live a reasonable life.

Our answer was a caravan, not the luxurious holiday home that the word caravan
brings to mind nowadays, but a flimsy hardboard and canvas affair, which I bought
from a farmer and parked at my old base, RAF Leeming. Heating and lighting were
primitive, when it rained I had to literally bail out the roof which tended to sag when
wet, and when the weather heated up, there was no insulation or ventilation.

Within the year Rosemary presented me with my first daughter, Julie, and we quickly
had to move out of our little honeymoon caravan. It was no place for a newborn baby
to live in. So it was back to Thirsk, to Rosemary's mother's house to live, and the
caravan was sold at a loss, a fore-runner of the many problems that were to
continually beset our family life and often threatened to destroy it completely.

But my instinctive trust in prayer, hope and belief, in other people and events, never
left me and I felt the increasing urge to learn and to fight my way to the top. The
pressures were starting to build.

Age 20 years

'Never give in, never give in, never ever give in'.
SIR WINSTON CHURCHILL

A little over three years later, Christine was born, to be followed after a similar interval by Beverley. As my family grew, so did my responsibilities, to cope with which the company I was working for sent me on a 'Time and Motion' study course at York, where I stayed for four months, followed by two years training on the job.

Imagine my situation. Only partially educated, I was thrown in with a group of experienced students who had enjoyed a far better education than I had. In those computerless days, they used slide rules as a matter of routine. I coped, and demonstrated once again my innate mathematical ability, by sitting up all night in my hotel bedroom teaching myself to work out the basis of slide rule technique without a tutor. I succeeded because I would not let myself do otherwise!

By 1962 I had assumed the responsibility of construction manager for my company and was in charge of millions of pounds worth of contracts, but was still living in the council house that we had acquired a few years earlier. When one of the directors called unexpectedly at my house one evening, he was horrified at someone in my position living where I did. The effect was two-fold. The company lent me the deposit to buy one of its own houses, so my family was better housed. But the pressures of my job, the mortgage payments, and the repayments on the loan caused an overload and I experienced my first panic attack or 'Anxiety State' which took five sorts of pills and eight months persistence to overcome.

If only I had known then, what art - the window on life - could do for me! But there was no one to advise me, and I doubt very much whether I would have accepted the idea of painting. Everything comes in its own good time, even if it does not seem so good at the time!

Barbados

'Where there is no imagination; there is horror'.
DOYLE

It is one thing to work for an organisation for a lengthy period; it is another altogether to feel that you are tied inexorably to them, which is what I experienced as I struggled to pay off the loan for the deposit on our house. In fact, I stayed for another 13 years altogether, only to find myself manoeuvred out of my position in a way that is only too familiar to those who study the machinations of big business.

To my mind, the business for which I held such a tremendous responsibility was successful and I was considered to be the most knowledgeable person in my trade in terms of experience and learning.

So to return to work after a well-earned holiday which had been intended to restore my full emotional health, only to be told that I was out of work, was a blow both to my self-esteem and to my plans for the family. It took three years to recover from that combination. By then (1968) Penny had joined the family, I was building my own house and was heavily committed financially, and I must have written to every construction company in the country before finally moving south. Like many immigrants to our new County, I did not like it at first, the insular attitude of the people, the unfamiliar surroundings. But that passed and here I am, settled in and feeling part of the local scene.

More problems meant that, finally, inevitably, I set up in business on my own and have stayed that way for nearly a quarter of a century.

Omar Homes Limited

'Things turn out best for the people who make the best out of the way things turn out'.
ART LINKLATER

The publishers wish to thank Omar Homes for the contribution they made towards the printing of this book.

With all this pressure; chasing; responsibilities; the unreliability of employers; the arrival of Emma in 1971, together with the demands of family life, it is not surprising that I once again experienced the problems of anxiety state. My brain became overloaded and promptly shut down most of its activities in the way that the local sub-station will if our demands on its electricity are too high.

The worst was yet to come, but following in its footsteps, so to speak, was, if not a remedy, at least a way of dealing with the trauma of Penny's sickness, our joint venture into the realms of artistic expression.

When she was just 16 years old, Penny suddenly displayed all the classic symptoms of schizophrenia as I have described elsewhere in this book. Who can tell what the real causes are for these dreadful character changes? All we can point to is what might have been the immediate trigger, bullying at school, the problems of adolescence for a young girl, any one of twenty or more causes could be credibly offered.

Whatever the cause, Penny went happily on holiday with her mother to the North of England, only to spend six weeks in hospital as her problems were diagnosed and a regime of treatment instituted.

Over the years my daughter has suffered six major attacks of her illness, with the result that the lives of everyone around her have been cruelly affected, her mother most of all. Rosemary has had major heart surgery and suffers from chronic anxiety and sleeplessness. Penny's sisters have all felt the strain and given their support in their various ways as, one at a time, the family's dreams have been shattered and our future path obscured by a relentless nightmare - the knowledge that at present there is no definitive cure for schizophrenia.

Then came the prospect of relief. A breath of fresh air; a ray of warm sunshine; a
welcome spring shower - these are all images that spring to mind when I look back at
Penny's discovery of painting, for communication can be an almost impossible task
for many sufferers of this much misunderstood illness and in her paintings, executed
with loving care and a patient attention to detail that one would hardly expect from a
victim of mental disorder, Penny has learned to reveal her emotions and the true
sensitivity of her feminine soul. She really is a lovely girl.

She shows neither anger nor resentment, but a warm, all-embracing love for nature in
its most intimate expression. Look, for example, at the vivacious bouquet of flowers in
a be-ribboned basket entitled 'Mother's Day' that Penny produced in 1996; the
exquisite floral arrangements, the acutely observed colouring, the exuberance of it all.
Study her water colour of the same year, 'Remembrance', of poppies with a
counterpoint of daisies and a rich accompaniment of greens and blues.

These are expressions of love, of life, of warmth. The real Penny, who lives imprisoned
behind the facade of schizophrenic despair.

Imagine then, with what trepidation I decided to risk the embarrassment of failure and
at the age when most men retire from work, hesitantly stroke canvass with a
paintbrush for the very first time!

My own paintings are produced in a much shorter time and with far less attention to
detail than my daughter's. Yet we have worked together in spirit. The young girl that I
had thought was lost to me for ever having metamorphosed into a caring woman
whose personal anguish has been made explicit - and with it comes a complete
mutual understanding that no other form of communication could ever have achieved.

Chapter Five   Sunshine - Father

One word, which has been used again and again by art lovers and critics to whom I have shown some of my work, is 'naive'. But in each case it was intended as a compliment, almost as a school of painting, following on from the various 'isms' of Expressionism, Pointillism, Modernism and so on. My Naivetism has been my reply to the cruelly complicated world of personality disorder, and following my paintings over the three short years since I first put brush to paper, I can trace the progress of Penny's illness.

Bad patches followed by the false dawn of partial remission, joyful moments cut off all too soon by the remorseless onslaught of an unexpected breakdown - all are there to be seen and understood by those who know.

And what of the panic attacks, as I prefer to call them. An introduction to stress management whioh I was given by an experienced and understanding psychological nurse has proved invaluable in loosening tightened chest muscles, slackening off the strangling effects of emotional despair and restoring hope. But it is only through my paintings that I shall finally be able to explain clearly and concisely my true belief in prayer and hope for the final release of doubt.

Where does this leave Penny - and the thousands of others who, like her, are the victims of an unseen and unexplained aggressor?

At 32, my daughter has all the looks of a lively 21 year old. Her long hair is carried with style, her beauty is of the sort to make anyone look and look again, and her positive personality, incredibly and stubbornly positive in the face of her disability, makes one aware of the power of the human personality in the face of incredible odds.

Not only does she paint, but Penny's ability with a sewing needle has even been demonstrated on television where she has shown examples of perfect patchwork and cross-stitching.

Where Penny has ventured, others could follow, and as more advanced medication is being constantly researched and tested, sufferers from schizophrenia can hope to live their lives more fully from year to year until the ultimate cure will banish the disease into the realms of medical history.

Why, oh why can the world's medical profession not deliver us salvation from our suffering? Penny and I pray together for deliverance from schizophrenia.

I suppose if you consider your own job or profession, you will accept that you have become very familiar with your role and the things that you do. When you are dealing with people however, that familiarity can be quite daunting. For example the airline pilot knows that the storm he is flying through is quite safe and really a mere squall. To the nervous passenger, eyeing the black sky, swirling clouds and electric flashes, it is a tempest with all the might and power to snatch him from the safety of his seat and dash him, lifeless against the hillside almost a mile below him.

We found psychiatrists to be just like that. To us, our worst fears had been realised when the illness was diagnosed, yet in reality, when Penny is well, she is capable of the most rewarding and profound love and affection. Very much a daddy's girl as a child, Penny's life has been simplified by her illness. She does not have to worry about a job, for as yet, she is not ready to make that commitment. Equally, although she yearns to become a true women and find the love of a man, her closest relationship remains that with her parents and her sisters.

Like those squalls, Penny's outbursts of emotion are varied and transient. Love and regret follow anger and frustration. That purity and simplicity of emotion, developed over fifteen years of illness have given our Penny an almost serene personality. The real Penny, beneath those emotional weather fronts, that pass so quickly, is beautiful and calm, similar perhaps to one who has shunned society to join a closed order.

Again, like that flight through the storm, our fears about schizophrenia are largely unfounded and based on our own emotions and fears, rather than on fact. Why are we so irrational when we are what is considered 'normal' and so at peace when we are considered ill?

Sea and Sun

'The unendurable is the beginning of the curve of joy'.
DUUNA BARNES

Schizophrenics, like the weather, rarely harm anyone and although the media would have us believe otherwise, violence towards others is rare. The sufferer is in reality more at war with themselves than others, and any aggression manifests itself as self-harm, rather than attacks on others.

In reality, most individuals with this condition prefer to withdraw and spend time on their own, away from other people and the carer's challenge is to stimulate interest and encourage the person to play a more active role.

Of course we can perhaps forgive the pilot for forgetting to reassure us when the plane hits that squall. He may rightly assume that most on the plane are experienced passengers who have seen the phenomena before and know that the storm will pass and their journey will not be disrupted.

For us, and countless others like us, we had little knowledge about mental illness and schizophrenia was a word we could barely spell, let alone interpret. Yet for us, the psychiatrist's words were received like a safety announcement on a plane - we did not really listen as we were too busy worrying about the dark clouds and turbulence ahead. Resources are scarce in the National Health Service and although things might be different in other countries, we felt very alone at the time.

Lazy days

'Things do not change; we change'.
HENRY DAVID THOREAU

There were many questions we wanted to ask but, to be honest, we felt selfish asking them - after all, this man was very busy and our biggest feelings were of guilt and fear; surely, we should be asking how to make our Penny better?

Schizophrenia is well researched and understood, with much knowledge amassed in the 90 years since the condition was first diagnosed. What a pity that more is not shared outside professional circles. It's rather like when you are afraid on that plane, flying through the storm. Your hands go clammy and your heart thumps - yet you try really hard not to let the person sitting beside you know that you're afraid. The truth however, is that usually they're afraid too, and trying to hide that fact from you! Think how much better it would be if you could share your fear, hold hands and face the challenge together.

The first thing that any parent thinks when their child is diagnosed with a mental illness is that it must in some way be their fault. Those feelings of guilt almost equal the feelings of despair and the fear. Physical conditions although equally distressing are easier to comprehend. You can often actually see what the problem is and can certainly relate the recovery to well established benchmarks. We all know how quickly to expect a wound to heal, or a bone to mend, or a bacterial infection to be conquered by antibiotics.

With mental illnesses and in particular with schizophrenia, there are no real benchmarks and healing can take a few weeks or years.

Block Island, New York

'The only way to discover the limits of the possible is to go beyond them, to the impossible'.
ARTHUR C CLARKE

To some extent, the parents can be blamed, but only if they themselves have suffered the illness. In fact there is a 10 per cent chance that the child of a schizophrenic will him or herself develop the illness at some time. That compares with the 1 per cent chance that you have if you have no family history of the illness.

Behaviourally, there is no link between upbringing and the illness. Again, we all would like to spend more time with our children, but inevitably, they arrive at a time when our lives are dominated by career and in my case, building a successful business. Much of my feeling of guilt about Penny's illness stemmed from my fear that I had neglected her during those early years, when work was all I really had time for - how I wish I could have found a better way to manage my time in those days.

Despite my busy life, having five daughters did mean that on many occasions, it was impossible to ignore their demands for attention and as our family grew, we all became closer and closer. That bond, between parents and daughters, sister to sister remains strong in our family to this day and it is perhaps one of our greatest strengths that we have faced Penny's illness as a family, not a group of individuals.

All of our daughters live within ten miles of the family home, our eldest works with me in my business and we see them all several times a week. For Penny, having the love and support of her sisters is important and when independence for her becomes a reality, rather than a dream, she will have ready and rapid access to help in every aspect of her life.

Broads

'From here to eternity'.
JAMES JONES

For others, where family ties are not so strong, the illness can go undiagnosed for years. It is unlikely that anyone will wake up one morning, feel 'schizophrenic' and call the doctor! The hallucinations, voices and other symptoms appear disturbing but horribly real to the sufferer. Many therefore seek help on their own and it needs the encouragement and cajoling of friends, family and neighbours to take that first step towards getting help.

Even once treatment has commenced, there is nothing to prevent the sufferer from stopping their medication, failing to keep hospital appointments and becoming more confused and psychotic. This is why so many mentally ill people end up living on the streets - they cannot make sense of their world and the fabric of normal life disintegrates - society steps around their needs and they find themselves desperate, cold and very alone.

Returning to our plane, if it did crash, the survivors would know they were injured and rescuers would be able to make a rapid diagnosis and provide emergency treatment - right there on that hillside. With schizophrenia, although the breakdown that sparks the illness can be just as traumatic, its treatment is far from simple.

Fishing

After V. Parkhurst

'He who has begun his task has half done it'.
HORACE

Children in a playground, running, dancing, skipping, shouting; in the corner, by the railings, one is quiet, looking out, away from the school - the other children run around her, tugging at her scarf. She stands there like a tree surrounded by snow flurries - a tear slowly emerges and rolls down her chilled cheek.

'Why won't they leave me alone' she thinks, 'why can't I be just like everybody else?'

The bell rings, the laughter stops, the children rush in to school, falling over themselves as they scramble to hang up their coats, each on its own peg, with the name of the child in bright colours written underneath. Last in, is that quiet girl from by the railings, slowly she follows her classmates and hangs her coat last. When she reaches the classroom the lesson has started.

'Late again' scolds the teacher.' Why can't you learn to listen for the bell like all the others', she adds. The arc of her swinging arm points out rows of giggling children, all of her enemies are once more relishing in her misery.

'Why, oh why,' she reflects, 'was I born to be different - how I wish I was grown up and away from this place.

Single bird

'And I was filled with such delight as prisoned birds must find in freedom'.
SIEGFREID SASSOON

Schizophrenia is not recognised as the product of those playground bullies, but for our Penny, we are sure it was a major contributor. There is no logic as to why bullies pick on any particular individual. What is known, is that the bullied suffer long after their school days and on into adulthood. The knocks that your self-esteem takes in those innocent childhood pranks are only now being recognised as a major factor in adult underachievement.

Surveys have shown that many of those who were bullied often give serious thought to suicide. In fact one survey showed that almost half had contemplated ending their lives. By comparison, those who had never been bullied, considered suicide much less frequently with fewer than one in a hundred giving much thought to this grisly solution to life's challenges.

Research shows that many who are bullied leave school the moment they are able, sacrificing further study and qualifications to avoid further pain and distress. Bullying often starts when a child moves from the cosy 'family' style environment of primary education to the bigger, harsher world of secondary schools. Although bullying is usually carried out by children of the same age, the environmental change as well perhaps as the influence of adolescent elders, creates a breeding ground for bullying.

Lighthouse

After L. Cochrane

'Grant me, O God, the power to see, in every storm the legacy of rainbows smiling down at me!'
VIRGINIA WUERFEL

The impact of bullying should never be underestimated. It causes the sufferer to question every aspect of their whole being. Normality becomes confused with abnormality. People question their gender, their intellect, their ability their preferences in every aspect of their lives. Yes, it is possible that some will use bullying as a justification for anything that they feel needs justification, but the fact remains that bullying can leave lasting scars.

Penny was a happy, quiet child, for whom the transition to senior school was difficult. A few miles from home, with children she did not know, our daughter found life difficult and although she hated school and the bullies who tormented her, she kept her unhappiness to herself and gave us little indication that things were not going well for her.

As a sensitive, caring person, Penny found it difficult to understand why people wanted to be cruel to her. Like many who are bullied, she assumed that she was at fault, different, flawed and in some way different from the rest. Otherwise why, she reasoned, would they taunt her so?

Chapter Seven Snow Flurries - School

Schooldays One

'Creativity represents a miraculous coming together of the uninhibited energy of the child'.
NORMAN PODHERTZ

It is known that girls bully girls in a far less physical way than boys bully boys. The lack of injury, or damage to property means that bullying is far harder to detect in daughters than sons. However, the verbal taunts, threats and goading meted out by girls can be just as damaging. There is frankly little truth in the old saying that 'sticks and stones will break your bones but words will never hurt you'. The fact is, that words can cut deeper than knives and cause wounds that take far longer to heal.

We honestly believe, although it is impossible to prove, that our Penny's illness, which started with that breakdown in Yorkshire at the age of 16, was brought about by bullying.

Like schizophrenia, being a victim of bullying is a lonely affair. Often, the people you tell about your bullying do not believe you, or handle it in an appropriate way. Teachers, parents and priests all have a tendency to belittle the problem.

'Do they hit you?' will be the question perhaps most will ask. 'No; then what's the problem then - act your age!' Believe me, that is not the right thing to say.

Holt Hall

'Peace be within thy walls'.
BOOK OF COMMON PRAYER

Only recently has it been recognised that those early knocks to your confidence and self-esteem last on throughout life. Think about the quiet, shy people you know who seem never to achieve all that they should in life. If the researchers are to be believed, their introversion probably results from bullying.

Why some are bullied and some become bullies is difficult to determine. Our Penny was quiet and shy, yet these traits alone should not be sufficient to warrant the unwelcome attention she endured. People can be targeted by bullies for a wide range of things; even children who have lost a parent through early death, are often bullied. Any vulnerability, real or perceived is rapidly picked on by mob and life for weeks, months or years becomes intolerable as the child becomes a victim - with a victim's outlook and expectation.

Schooldays Two

'Everyone has talent. What is rare is the courage to follow the talent to the dark place where it leads'.
ERICA JONG

Chapter Eight   Puddles - Sisters

96

Life is nothing more than a journey. We are born, we live and we die. Religious belief may give us hope, but physically our bodies follow a pre-determined path from tiny baby, through adulthood and on to old age. Have you ever stopped to realise how it is always so easy to guess the age of the people you meet? Yes, some may wear better than others, but it is rare that even cosmetics or surgery can fool you into thinking that someone is actually younger than they really are.

Our environment follows similar cycles, the lush green joy of Spring follows the cold starkness of Winter, only to wither in the heat of Summer and be mellowed and decayed in the damp of Autumn. Travel to foreign lands allows some of us to escape, if only for a while, from the natural cycle of nature but the seasons follow each other as surely as death follows life.

Storms, create change, impact, trauma, shock and bring about sudden change to our world. They override the seasonal norm, chilling and darkening a Summer afternoon or perhaps making the depths of Winter seem much deeper.

Shoes

'Walk cheerfully over the world'.
GEORGE FOX

Storms are rather like life itself. They arrive with impact, like the birth of a child. They change their surroundings, washing away the old, creating puddles and running torrents as the water they disgorge fights to escape from where it has been thrust. Those puddles and running rivulets remind me of children, urgent, anxious, demanding attention. As the power of the storm abates, the flow of water slows, having established its path and accepted its destiny. Then, when the clouds clear and the sun shines once more, the puddles dry up and disappear. Only the memory remains that where the dust now lies, once a small but mighty torrent raged. To me, families are like those storms and the children like those dancing puddles.

We were blessed with five daughters, the product of our very happy and vigorous marriage. Our love for each other has maintained the intensity of a storm for more than forty years. Like the storm, we know that one day our marriage will lose its strength as our lives come to their natural conclusion. However, unlike the puddles that result from the storm, our daughter Penny and her sisters, will continue to flourish after we are gone.

Again, like those puddles that grow and run together to form a little river, our daughters have grown together as we face the challenge of our Penny's illness. Each takes strength from the other and they all gladly give their support to their sister as she wrestles to make a recovery.

PRINCESS ELIZABETH 1st.

Princess Elizabeth

'To toast the Queen'.
DENIS HEALEY

100

Our first daughter, Julie was born in the summer of 1954 when we had been married less than a year. We were living with Rosemary's mother at the time as our small caravan was no place for a baby to live. I can remember the night only too well; that frantic ride, a mile down the road on my bike to the phonebox on the corner to call the ambulance. Then, back in the saddle and back to my beloved Rosemary. Sweet and helpless, with her mother holding her hand until I came back. My bladder seemed permanently full and I must have used the toilet seven times before the ambulance came out of the night and took us to hospital where Julie was born.

Strong and healthy, Julie now has her own family and has herself become a mother. She has three lively boys, who give us all so much pleasure, yet she remains a sister to Penny, supporting, encouraging and strengthening the bond between all of our daughters. Julie has a wonderful sense of humour and keeps us all smiling, even when those storm clouds are showering us with gloom with all of their might. Penny enjoys visiting Julie and her family, sharing a meal with her nephews and being an aunt.

Christine, our second daughter was born in December 1957 and is delightfully creative. Quieter than Julie, she is very sensitive and perceptive and is perhaps closer to Penny than most of us.

QUEEN ELIZABETH 1ST.

Queen Elizabeth

'The jewel in the crown'.
PAUL SCOTT

Clearly on the same wavelength, she actually shares the stress and tensions that so torment our Penny and thereby provides tremendous comfort in those dark and dismal hours when the storms are at their peak. Spirited, Christine was a rebellious teenager who gave us many sleepless nights and difficult moments as she emerged into womanhood and tested her feminine wiles on those around her. These experiences have made her a very strong character, confident and sure, yet sensitive and aware. Her son and three daughters reflect much of her character and she and her husband have formed a strong family unit that will outlive us and grow stronger as the years pass by.

Beverly followed a few years later, in March 1961 and again is very different from her sisters. For many years she worked with me in my company until a flaming row taught us both that working with family can have its disadvantages. Fortunately, we settled our differences and like the puddles merging and separating, are now very much in tune. Perhaps of all our girls, Beverly has my determination and she certainly shares my stubborn streak! She has a daughter of her own and will I suspect understand how we felt as she too will no doubt re-live the trauma of those teenage years as her own daughter grows up.

Penny is the subject of our book and, as you will by now appreciate, is a really unique person. Art and expression know no bounds where Penny is concerned. She is that shining light which emerges from the darkest sky, lowering a shaft of brilliant sunshine to point out to us all that from adversity comes that purity of life which only few will ever experience.

Jaws

'Man is the most formidable of all beasts of pray…the only one who prays systematically on its own species.'
WILLIAM JAMES

Our family was complete when Emma arrived in 1971. Seventeen years younger than Julie, Emma has always been the baby of the family and really, she always will be; certainly to Rosemary and me. Perhaps the closest to Penny, Emma spends much of her spare time with Penny and the two are real pals. Yet to get married, Emma shares her desire for marriage and motherhood with Penny. Both look forward to fulfilling their maternal instincts and raising a family as their sisters have done. Our family is already quite large, but as I increasingly reflect on my full and active life, I appreciate that when my storm passes and I am no more, those puddles I have created with my rain will last forever. My daughters' lives are changing and evolving, with their own children giving me a perspective on life and its meanings that no younger man could imagine. Life is good, but life is not constant. Nothing in life stays the same and we, mere mortals, appear, move, influence then disappear like so many puddles beside the road.

Is there more to life than birth, marriage and death? Penny's paintings, together with my own discovery of the medium of art, tell me that life has dimensions yet to be explored. Delights yet to be savoured and joys yet to be experienced. As Penny's illness continues to question our faith, we have to ask, what is life really all about?

Normans Reflections

After C. Cochrane

'The greater the contrast, the greater the potential'.
C G JUNG

Chapter Nine   Pearls

As the years rolled by my family became accustomed to the traumas, trials and tribulations of living with schizophrenia. Penny's health alternated between deep despair and the joys of virtual health. Her medication meant that even the good times were blunted by the powerful effect of the drugs and at times, I wondered if I would ever see my old Penny again, carefree, joyful and blessed with that wicked sense of humour.

Painting has been our salvation over the past few years and at times, it has been a time of great joy. Van Gogh too has been a great source of inspiration as we came to appreciate art. His experiences and talent helped us understand the force and feeling that can be focused through the brush and palette knife.

Although it was a chance remark by my art tutor at night school, who said our work resembled that of Van Gogh, the similarities between our lives is remarkable. The more I read of his life, the more of Penny's I see reflected in his earlier experience. As we move towards the conclusion of our book, where we have written of our life and feelings, we perhaps only differ from Van Gogh in that he did not have drugs to help him through his years of torment; neither was his condition understood. Writers can only hypothesise as to what drove him with such conviction down the tortured, self-sacrificing route to his eventual self destruction.

Iris

'There is only one success - to be able to spend your life in your own way'
CHRISTOPHER MORELY

One of six children (Penny is one of five) Van Gogh was a home loving introvert; his relationship with his parents was perhaps inhibited by his natural reluctance to push for attention. Rather like the smallest kitten in a litter, he only got what love and affection was left when his siblings' desires were sated.

I can't say the same was necessarily true of Penny. She was quiet, yes, but we tried to love and support all of our daughters equally. Did the demands of work, career and building my own business take my attentions away from her? I honestly don't know.

Equally, we can only guess that the shy, introvert Van Gogh was bullied at school. Certainly that was the cause of Penny's earliest illness and she seems so like Van Gogh that as kids don't change, he must have been bullied too.

Thrust into foreign lands by family pressure to succeed, Van Gogh led a lonely existence in London as a youth and stayed in Antwerp, Brussels, Italy and Paris as an artist. Yet everywhere he went, it seems his yearning for home drove his mind back to his family and the church in Holland where his father was pastor.

Fye Bridge

'A new life begins for us each and every second'.
JEROME K JEROME

He became preoccupied with religion in his early twenties and studied the Bible with a fervour that cannot have been equalled in history. He went out of his way to experience the things that he read. He gave to the needy and befriended the weak. He denied himself the few luxuries afforded by his spartan lifestyle. Bread and water became his staple diet and he chose to sleep on the floor rather than in his bed. As his odd behaviour became more apparent his family withdrew and he became increasingly alone in the world. Only his brother Theo remained supportive throughout his life.

Penny too has enjoyed the support of her sisters throughout her illness and like Van Gogh her paintings have been widely distributed within the pages of a calendar that my company distributes every Christmas. Unlike Van Gogh, Penny enjoys artistic acclaim during her lifetime!

Of course it would be self indulgent for me to make too many comparisons between my beloved daughter and Vincent Van Gogh, even though both seem to have suffered in the same way. Perhaps it is through their art that they are alike. That spark that drives their creativity is the shared irritant of schizophrenia.

I have taken considerable comfort over the years from an analogy that was popular with Van Gogh and which certainly helped me to understand the true spirit of Penny's illness and how in a macabre way it has been so important in giving her an artist's eye and talent.

Dreaming

'Live your beliefs and you can turn your world around'.
HENRY THOREAU

Think about the oyster and how it becomes irritated and disturbed by a piece of grit within its shell. How does it handle this? Why it creates a pearl! Ironic but true and remarkably appropriate when you look at any truly great artist, writer or musician. The stimuli for success are almost always traumatic in nature.

Schizophrenia, the condition that has plagued our Penny for years has inspired some of her greatest paintings. Vivid, stark and bursting with colour as her mind wrestles with itself. Frightened and lonely, with that horrible realisation that she is alone with her illness, the edges softened by medication. But the burning, driving, bursting hot core of anxiety driving her brush over canvas as she expresses her feelings in the way she has found to be best.

Van Gogh too was a frenetic painter, creating art with a ferocity equalled only by others considered 'ill at peace' with themselves and their society. Tell me, why is it that we respect the art, but choose not to seek an understanding of the artist? Perhaps in music, there are parallels we could explore. Much was written in the past for the artificially induced voice of the castrato and many boys unwittingly and unknowingly were sacrificed to a live devoid of sexual fulfilment, all in the name of art.

Our society demands extremes of endeavour to create art, food, music and more. Yet we remain largely ignorant and intolerant of those able to deliver the required result, because of some flaw or blemish about their character that gives them those highly valued skills. Is it society that is odd, or those who live within it? That question continues to haunt me as I examine every aspect of our lives in my search for the reasons for it and for the illness and the suffering we have all endured for all of these years.

Carribean Sunset

'When I look into the future, it's so bright, it burns my eyes'.
OPRAH WINFREY (BORN - 1954)

116

Van Gogh sought solace from his condition with the only real medication available to him. Self prescribed, he took liberal daily doses of wine, coffee and tobacco; two stimulants and one relaxant, perhaps not a bad combination. Do you drink to escape? Does coffee drive you through the day? Do you gasp for a cigarette when the pressure's on? Do you see again, how mental illness is nothing more than an exaggeration of normality?

Of course Van Gogh's illness was poorly treated as little was known at the time. Hot baths, cold cells and rejection by the community in which he lived, all compounded what we now would treat very differently.

We all know that Van Gogh mutilated himself, slicing off an earlobe in a manic attempt to build a relationship with women. We also perhaps know that he died two days after a bungled suicide attempt (or was it therefore successful?) with his beloved brother Theo by his side.

Thankfully our Penny shares none of that with Van Gogh and cherishes her life and the gifts with which she is endowed. In fact the opposite is almost true. Penny encourages me to paint and although I suffer from anxiety, my paintings lack the delicate detail of hers. We share the same ability to create dramatic images when troubled and at times, it can be hard to differentiate between the two. Alas, the sad fact is that because the piece of grit under Penny's shell is bigger than mine, so too are the artistic pearls she creates

The Cottage

'Whatever you can do, or dream you can, begin it. Boldness has genius, power
and magic in it. BEGIN IT NOW'.
GOETHE

Chapter Ten   Boughs

Trees, like people, start life small and tender. Age and the experiences of life weather and shape them. Think of those avenues of trees you see on hilltops, twisted and bent by the prevailing wind, misshapen and bent, yet retaining their strength.

Equally fascinating are the Japanese bonsai trees; constant pruning and clipping prevents them from realising their natural potential and they reach maturity stunted and short.

Many times I have walked with Penny in the countryside near our home; misty autumn days when the wind never seems to stop and the trees sway and creak as each gust pushes, pulls and twists the ancient boughs.

Storms put additional strains on the trees, breaking off weak or damaged limbs. In great storms huge branches are torn from the trunks and trees that are old sometimes succumb totally and collapse.

How similar we are to those trees. As I have gone through my life the wailing wind of Penny's illness has distorted my perspective and twisted my mind as I search for answers in the face of the onslaught of the raging torment of her illness. Yet at other times, I sway gently with the mood, enjoy basking in the sunshine of our love and Penny's deep and profound vision of the world expressed through her beautiful paintings.

Five minutes

'In search of lost time'.
MARCEL PROUST

Anxiety as a parent is a natural phenomenon and like any parent, I care about all of my children; all five of them, lovely daughters – each as individual as the trees that surround my garden. Rosemary and I are of course older and less resilient, worn by the tempests of Penny's mind.

Over the years I have experienced real depression myself as I wonder what the future will bring. Hope, fear, the unknown, the worst, the best, the highs, the lows, all fight and focus my mind as I also wrestle with the complexities of running my successful business.

The ability to relax, without resort to the sedative, short-term effects of alcohol, is a skill I only discovered late in life. The secret I have found is to isolate myself from the cause of my distress, gradually, slowly and effectively. To be frank with you, at the outset I was sceptical, but as I shared my experiences with others, I found that panic attacks and other manifestations of anxiety were common amongst men.

A good friend of mine, with a wonderful family, successful business and healthy life finds that, because he is never satisfied with what he has achieved and is constantly seeking more, anxiety provokes raging migraine attacks which hit him when he tries to relax. On holiday or at the weekend he is often confined to bed by blinding headaches, nausea and problems with his vision. When the flow of adrenaline is interrupted by a break from his office, he literally collapses into a heap on his bed, unable to move for several hours. The harder he works the worse they become when he stops. Ask yourself, is this good for him or his family? No, of course it isn't. I shared with him the technique I will shortly share with you. I can tell you, I thought he would laugh, as he is a very direct and abrupt type of chap. He tried the technique and believes that it has helped him. It could help you too!

This way

'Always someone else's horizon. Oh bliss!'
KENNETH GRAHAM

Here is what you do: it is really quite simple. You need to free up an hour of time and find a place where you will not be disturbed. Perhaps in front of the fire on a winter's evening, when the wind is howling outside and you are snug and safe in your living room.

Sit in your favourite chair and make yourself comfortable. (It might help to have a drink and go to the toilet first, so that physical needs do not impact on your mental relaxation!). Slowly become aware of your body and think about how each part moves and works. Control your breathing, in other words, switch off your body's 'autopilot' and take the controls.

OK, so you are now at the helm of your ship, your body, your home for the duration of your life. Now, doesn't it feel better already?

What you have to do is focus your whole mind on each part of your body in turn. Tighten, then relax; tighten then relax; repeat this a few times and then move on. Fingers, wrists, arms, shoulders, toes, legs, torso, neck and head. Even your ears if you're lucky enough to be able to waggle them!

Your breathing must become modulated and controlled and it helps to push your chest out as you breath in, then let it fall as you breathe out. Gently, slowly, relaxation takes time and is as you might expect very restful.

Autumn

'Now it is Autumn and the falling fruit'.
D H LAWRENCE

If like me, you find that at times it all gets a bit too much, you can use this technique sitting at your desk. At times, when the pressure's really on, I find I cannot breathe and almost choke on my own fear and frustration. Believe me, switching off the phone, turning down the light and taking it easy helps you overcome the momentary panic and focus your mind on all that is positive. My troubles revolve around my daughter and her illness, my friend's, on his inability to see his own good fortune in his headlong flight towards greater achievement.

Whatever drives you, take time out to relax and literally unwind your body. Remember the trees and those boughs that form their structure. Constant wind will weaken the branches and unless the tree has faced that prevailing wind as it has grown, it will not have the strength to overcome the sudden gusts that can accompany a storm.

In England in 1987 we had a great storm that tore across our landscape and tore many trees out from the ground. Even now as I write this book ten years later, the scars remain on our landscape where many fine trees were toppled and fell. We, as people are no different. If there were to be a schizophrenia epidemic, like those flu epidemics of years gone by, we would see the lasting scars caused by that storm, not on trees, but on people torn from normality by shock, stress and trauma.

Isn't it strange how we are quick to prop up trees when age and infirmity trouble them, yet we seem never to recognise that people are just the same. Our Penny has stood up well to her illness in many ways and at times is as happy as a lark in springtime. Her illness has over the years enabled her to develop a real resilience and her mind is flexible enough to bounce back from the deepest depression to relative joy.

Trees in wind

'Even if I knew that tomorrow the world would go to pieces, I would still plant
my apple tree'.
MARTIN LUTHER (1483 - 1546)

Those of us who do not experience long term illness personally are less fortunate and our minds can become very brittle and can snap very easily should a sudden gust of stress strike unexpectedly.

So strange to share the experience of stress and to find that the ill are better able to cope than those considered well! Perhaps once again it will encourage you to challenge your perception of 'well-ness' and illness. Think about it; which is really which and is there really a line between the two?

Picnic

Painting is a Journey into the Unknown
NORMAN O'NEILL.

After S.J. Derbishire

Chapter Eleven   Sunset

As I grow older my quest to understand the reasons behind Penny's illness becomes more urgent. I have no desire to leave this world until I really know why. Why should such a cruel illness afflict someone so special? Why us? How many times did I reflect on this matter?

Of course we are all accused of seeking the meaning of life as we move into its final chapter, but I perhaps more than many, really did feel the need to understand just where all this pain was leading. Our family had started out in the wild hinterland between the North Yorkshire moors and the Dales. An area marked now by the A1, our country's oldest and longest main thoroughfare, along which every day, thousands rush from North to South and back again. Do they know why they are making that journey?

Yes they do, but I bet you they don't stop to think. Is it really important? Will it really matter? In my experience, few will even consider for a fleeting moment, why am I making this journey at all. Life is to be lived; yet for many, it is lived as if driven by clockwork, beating hearts and driving minds, spurred on by transient ambition and passing whim. Our Penny has taken a by-pass and avoided those issues since that fateful day when she suffered her first breakdown in that field near Northallerton. She has focused her life on herself, on recovering from her illness and by painting what she sees and what she feels, her journey through life is so bright and pure.

Church

'Our existence is but a brief crack of light between the eternities of darkness'.
VLADIMIC NABOKOV

I can remember one autumn afternoon, we were all at home in our village, a place where some 600 people reside. It was one of those bright, crisp afternoons when the leaves almost glow on the trees, changing, weakening, falling to the ground at the slightest rustle in the breeze.

Penny and I were in our garden, Rosemary had gone out shopping and all was very still. A plume of sweet scented smoke spiralled up from the bonfire we were making from the leaves. I remember we talked about hedgehogs and how we looked and laughed as we checked none were under the pile of twigs and leaves before I struck the match that lit the fire.

Like the match, our Penny was quick to flame and for some reason, she decided to take off and ran off through the village. I waited a while then followed her, anxious to calm her and bring her home. There was a dampness in the air and the smoke from my fire was white and dense. Even when I turned the corner, I could smell the fire on my shirt.

Man and dog

After G. Lees

'Keep your face to the sunshine, and you cannot see the shadow'.
HELEN KELLER (1880 - 1968)

In the centre of our village stands a church. It is an ancient building with a round tower built of flint. We had been there many times, but really, had never looked on ourselves as being particularly religious. I paused by the gate, catching my breath and wondering where our Penny had gone. The church door, a heavy oak affair, was slightly open and I walked through the churchyard and went inside. The stillness of the air was disturbed only by the distant sound of passing traffic and the waning autumn sun shone its rich yellow rays through the stained glass window.

In front of the altar knelt our Penny, hands gripping the rail and staring at the cross on the altar. I moved up the aisle and knelt down beside her. Neither of us spoke but I think we both knew, then if never before, that hope was the secret of eternal salvation. Hope that life would not be fruitless, that any achievement, however small, was preferable to inertia.

Is there really a God, caring for us, watching over us, protecting us from evil? Why then was schizophrenia creating such chaos in our lives? What purpose did it have? We both knelt and prayed for what seemed like an eternity. Our love for each other and our shared desire for peace made that moment for me, one of the most intensely emotional experiences of my life.

Ploughing

'Today is the first day of the rest of your life'.
DALE CARNEGIE

Calmed and content, we walked home again, we held hands, still not speaking but knowing in our hearts that we had found something special in that church. We had discovered that faith, focused on God or not, was the route to happiness and understanding.

From that day on, faith played a greater part in my conscious life. I realised that we have to care for each other and even those we do not know. The most precious commodity is life itself. Do those scurrying drivers traversing the country on the A1 motorway really understand that? I suspect not.

Through our art, Penny and I found true contentment and appreciated that although others might not understand, we could both express the most personal of feelings with the help of paper, paint and a brush. Like Van Gogh, I wrestled at times to express the emotions that burst from my mind like exploding rainbows. Penny too, had times when it was only her painting that kept her going. The intensity of her pictures, the detail the almost fanatical desire to represent every last feature of the image burning in her mind was fantastic to witness.

Bamboo I

'I think that I will never see, a poem as lovely as a tree'.
JOYCE KILMEC

140

Through my own art, my own torment and frustration as a caring father, I knew that I had soaked up many of the symptoms of Penny's illness, removing the pain from my daughter's mind as if I was mopping the perspiration from her fevered brow. Anxiety drove me to consult doctors about my own mental health and at times, safety could only be sought with the help of a bottle of little red pills. With Penny, I suffered, with Penny I fought, with the deep and calming love of my wife Rosemary, we both recovered, we both took comfort from her care, her love and her loyalty.

Through sharing this book, reading my words and seeing our pictures, you have, dear reader, gained a glimpse of the passion for understanding that has racked both Penny and me for many long years. I hope that you will think differently of those with mental illness, understand that anxiety is a natural response and appreciate that the only difference between schizophrenia and a broken arm is the speed and certainty of recovery.

Bamboo II

'Hope deffered maketh the heart sick, but when the desire cometh, it is a tree of life'.
PROVERBS, (BIBLE)

You may believe in God, you may believe in a different God to Penny and I, or you may remain sceptical. Through the images on these pages, we hope you will discover something, however small, that gives you the peace and tranquillity we all deserve. Read, study, share and enjoy, today, tomorrow and whenever you feel the need to reflect, consider and look forward. One day when the sun will set on your very existence and the dark storms of death will carry you across the sky, you will be forced to reflect on the things that you have done. I pray, do all that you can to leave your light shining brightly in our uncertain and unyielding world when you are gone.

Broads sailing

'*I don't think of all the misery, but all the beauty that still remains*'.
ANNE FRANK (1929 - 1945)

Now, you have reached the end of my book, but of course the story is far from over. As I write these words, I reflect on my life and the illness that has haunted my beloved daughter's life.

There is much to be thankful for; her physical health, her love, her wonderful sense of humour and of course her paintings. Like me, you have enjoyed her art, (as well perhaps as mine!), and will appreciate the power of the feelings that have driven us both to pick up the brush and express our feelings on canvas and board.

As time goes by, Penny's control of her illness improves and I can see the day when she will lead what we would call a normal family life. My dream is that she will meet a young doctor and fall in love. Penny, like any woman wants to have children and we, as her parents, look forward to the day when she adds to our large family.

Penny, like all of our daughters, has inherited my determination and drive and will I am confident look back on her illness one day as just a chapter in a long and satisfying life. God bless her, and you my friend for reading my story and opening your mind to the realities of schizophrenia and the tremendous force that drives us all to express ourselves and influence those around us.

Sunset III

'When the sun goes down with a flaming ray'.
CARRIE BOND

Hat and Pipe

After Vincent Van Gogh

'*Laughter means health*'.
NORMAN O'NEILL

Vincent Van Gogh

After Vincent Van Gogh

Determination means success
NORMAN O' NEILL

Sunset II

'When you feel low think of all the positive things you have done'.
NORMAN O' NEILL

Lamplight

After C. Cochrane

'Every lamp that I pass is a light to the future'.
NORMAN O'NEILL

Cathedral II

'Losing a loved one means thinking how to go forward yourself to live life to the full'.
NORMAN O'NEILL

Blue butterfly

'Life is made up of small pleasures'.
NORMAN LEAR

Thing   *After C. Cochrane*

'You die if you worry, you die if you don't, so why worry at all'.
NORMAN O'NEILL

Sunflower and friends

After G. O'Keefe

'The secret of success is making your vocation your vocation'.
MARK TWAIN

Tranquility

After C. Cochrane

Positive Thinking the Way Forward
NORMAN O'NEILL

Italy

'Where there is no vision, people perish'.
PROVERBS 29:18

Picture Index